LangChain & LlamaIndex: A Practical Guide

Contents

Part 1: Introduction to Large Language Models (LLMs)

Chapter 1: What are Large Language Models (LLMs)?

Imagine a computer program that can have a conversation with you, translate languages fluently, write different kinds of creative content, and answer your questions in an informative way. This is the magic of Large Language Models (LLMs).

1.1 Demystifying LLMs

LLMs are a type of artificial intelligence (AI) program focused on understanding and generating human language. They achieve this by being trained on massive amounts of text data, like books, articles, code, and even online conversations. This training allows them to learn the patterns and statistical relationships between words, enabling them to perform various tasks related to language.

1.2 How do LLMs Work?

Think of an LLM like a student who gets really good at predicting the next word in a sentence after reading millions of books. They don't necessarily understand the deep meaning of everything they read, but they can

recognize patterns and use those patterns to generate similar text or

complete tasks.

Here's a simplified breakdown:

- **Training:** LLMs are trained on massive datasets using a technique

  called deep learning. This involves complex algorithms processing

  the text data, identifying patterns, and learning relationships

  between words.

- **Neural Networks:** Deep learning relies on artificial neural networks,

  inspired by the human brain. These networks consist of

  interconnected layers that process information and learn from the

  data.

- **Prediction:** During training, the LLM learns to predict the next word

  in a sequence based on the preceding words. This ability to predict

  allows the LLM to generate human-like text, translate languages,

  and perform other language-related tasks.

1.3 Key Characteristics of LLMs

- **Large Scale:** As the name suggests, LLMs are massive models requiring significant computing power and vast amounts of data for training.

- **Statistical Learning:** LLMs learn statistical patterns in language, not necessarily the meaning behind the words.

- **Versatility:** LLMs can be used for various tasks, including:

  - Text generation: Creating different kinds of creative text formats, like poems, code, scripts, musical pieces, etc.

  - Machine translation: Translating text from one language to another.

  - Text summarization: Condensing lengthy text into a shorter, informative summary.

  - Question answering: Providing informative answers to user queries.

  - Chatbots: Powering chatbots that can converse with users in a natural way.

- **Continuous Learning:** LLMs can be further fine-tuned and improved by exposing them to new data.

Chapter 2: Applications of LLMs

LLMs are revolutionizing how we interact with computers and information. Here are some exciting applications across various fields:

2.1 Communication and Creativity

- **Machine Translation:** LLMs are breaking down language barriers by enabling real-time, high-quality translation between languages. This can be used for tasks like translating foreign news articles, documents, or even live conversations.

- **Chatbots and Customer Service:** LLMs are powering chatbots that can answer customer queries, provide support, and even handle simple transactions. This can improve customer service efficiency and personalize user experiences.

- **Content Creation:** From writing different creative text formats like poems or scripts to generating marketing copy or product descriptions, LLMs can assist humans in content creation tasks.

2.2 Education and Research

- **Personalized Learning:** LLMs can personalize learning experiences by tailoring educational content to individual student needs and learning styles.

- **Research Assistance:** LLMs can be used as research assistants, helping scientists analyze vast amounts of data and identify patterns or trends.

2.3 Business and Productivity

- **Email and Document Summarization:** LLMs can quickly summarize lengthy emails and documents, allowing users to grasp key information efficiently.

- **Code Generation and Review:** LLMs can assist programmers by generating code snippets or even complete functions based on specific requirements. They can also help review code for potential errors.

2.4 Examples and Case Studies

- **Case Study: Multilingual Customer Service:** A travel company uses an LLM-powered chatbot to answer customer queries in multiple languages, providing 24/7 support to a global audience.

- **Example: AI-powered Writing Assistant:** A writer uses an LLM-powered writing assistant to brainstorm content ideas, check for grammar errors, and even suggest different writing styles.

These are just a few examples of how LLMs are being applied in various fields. As LLM technology continues to evolve, we can expect even more innovative applications to emerge in the future.

Part 2: Building LLM-powered Applications

Chapter 3: Introduction to LLM Frameworks

Imagine you want to build a house. You could gather all the necessary materials (bricks, wood, nails) and try to build it yourself. But wouldn't it be easier and more efficient to use a pre-built framework like Legos? LLM frameworks work similarly.

LLM frameworks are software tools that provide a structured environment for developers to build applications powered by Large Language Models (LLMs). These frameworks offer essential functionalities like:

- **Interaction with LLMs:** They simplify communication between your application and the LLM, handling tasks like sending prompts and receiving responses.
- **Data Management:** They help manage and organize the data used by the LLM, including user input and relevant information for generating responses.
- **Customization:** Frameworks allow developers to tailor the LLM's behavior to their specific application needs.

Using an LLM framework streamlines the development process, saving developers time and effort compared to building everything from scratch There are several LLM frameworks available, each with its strengths and weaknesses. Two popular options are LangChain and LlamaIndex, which we'll explore in detail in the following chapters.

Building Complex Query Pipelines

LangChain and LlamaIndex enable developers to craft intricate pipelines that process and retrieve information efficiently. These pipelines can handle diverse tasks such as multi-step queries, hybrid search strategies, and conditional logic for AI workflows. Here, we delve into constructing robust pipelines, leveraging advanced functionalities of both tools to integrate seamlessly into your application stack.

One of the hallmarks of advanced query pipelines is the ability to work with structured and unstructured data simultaneously. For instance, you might retrieve insights from a structured database while parsing unstructured text data from articles or reports. LangChain's prompt chaining capabilities complement LlamaIndex's indices, allowing for dynamic query construction.

Consider a scenario: an e-commerce company wants to answer user queries about product availability and reviews. The system first checks inventory data (structured), then supplements the response with review summaries from user-generated content (unstructured). A pipeline for this scenario might look like:

1. **Step 1: Inventory Check**

   Query the SQL database with LangChain's SQLDatabaseChain. This involves generating a prompt dynamically based on user inputs, executing it via the SQL engine, and processing the results for downstream tasks.

2. **Step 2: Review Summaries**

   Use LlamaIndex to retrieve relevant sections from customer reviews indexed in a document database. Implement hybrid search (combining keyword and semantic) to ensure high relevance.

3. **Step 3: Integration and Final Response**

   Combine the outputs using LangChain's OutputParser to format a coherent and actionable response. The ability to transform structured results and free-text into a user-friendly summary underscores the pipeline's robustness.

Implementing these workflows requires granular control over prompt engineering, data preprocessing, and error handling. LangChain's Transformers integrations and LlamaIndex's embeddings-based retrieval allow developers to construct pipelines with minimal latency and high accuracy.

Advanced Retrieval Techniques with LlamaIndex

LlamaIndex is a powerful tool for enhancing information retrieval, especially for large datasets. Beyond simple retrieval, its capabilities in embeddings-based search, query expansion, and cross-encoder integrations elevate its utility in advanced systems. In this chapter, we explore cutting-edge techniques that leverage these functionalities.

Multi-Vector Query Strategy

Instead of relying on a single vector representation of queries, advanced retrieval involves multiple vectors representing different semantic facets of the query. For example, a query like *"Best smartphones under $500 with good cameras"* might break into:

- Budget constraints: "$500"
- Product category: "smartphones"
- Feature-specific preferences: "good cameras"

Each component is embedded into a separate vector using LlamaIndex's custom embedding models, enabling fine-grained retrieval. These vectors can then be scored independently against document embeddings, and the results merged dynamically to return nuanced responses.

Temporal Retrieval Augmentation

Many domains require retrieving contextually relevant information based on time. Temporal retrieval allows for prioritizing documents or sections with timestamps closest to the query context. LlamaIndex supports metadata filtering, which can incorporate date constraints into queries. For example, when processing news articles about "economic policies," temporal filters ensure that only recent data is prioritized.

Enhanced Context Expansion

Combining LangChain and LlamaIndex, developers can implement context expansion techniques where the query scope dynamically broadens based on initial retrieval results. Suppose a query fails to produce a sufficient match. In that case, LangChain's prompt engineering modules can generate follow-up queries by rephrasing or generalizing the input, while LlamaIndex ensures the expanded context doesn't introduce noise.

Seamless Multi-Model Integration

As enterprises increasingly adopt AI, there's a growing need to integrate multiple AI models for varied tasks. LangChain's model-agnostic design and LlamaIndex's indexing flexibility provide a foundation for seamless multi-model systems. This chapter explores the mechanics of combining models, optimizing query routing, and creating intelligent workflows that maximize the strengths of each model.

A real-world example involves integrating:

1. **LLMs for Natural Language Understanding (NLU)**
2. **Domain-specific models for knowledge-intensive tasks**
3. **Generative models for synthesizing outputs**

Imagine a medical application that diagnoses diseases. The system might:

- Use an LLM to parse patient symptoms.
- Query a domain-trained model for specific diagnostics.
- Use LangChain to chain these outputs and craft a human-readable report.

To optimize multi-model workflows:

- Implement **query routing logic** using LangChain's RouterChain. For example, based on user input, direct the query to the most relevant model.

- Use **parallel processing** where applicable. LlamaIndex allows simultaneous querying across indices (e.g., a biomedical paper repository and an EHR database).

- Design **feedback loops** using LangChain's memory modules, capturing interactions to fine-tune model responses dynamically.

Ensuring interoperability between models often requires preprocessing, like aligning tokenization schemes or unifying output formats. LangChain's utilities, combined with LlamaIndex's customizable indexing pipelines, streamline these challenges.

Real-Time AI Applications

Many AI systems demand real-time capabilities, from conversational agents to fraud detection engines. Achieving this requires optimizing every component, from data ingestion and indexing to query execution and response generation. LangChain and LlamaIndex are invaluable for building systems that scale in real-time.

Dynamic Memory Management

LangChain's memory modules enable tracking conversational state and context, even over long sessions. However, in real-time applications, memory optimization is crucial. Using **ephemeral memory chains**, developers can retain only critical context, reducing computational overhead without compromising response quality.

For example, in customer service chatbots, ephemeral memory can track the issue's context while discarding irrelevant back-and-forth. This improves speed while maintaining contextually accurate responses.

Optimizing LlamaIndex for Speed

LlamaIndex's indexing and retrieval capabilities can be fine-tuned for real-time applications:

- Use **incremental indexing** for streaming data. For instance, if new articles are continuously added to a knowledge base, incremental updates prevent the need for full re-indexing.

- Pre-compute embeddings for commonly accessed documents, reducing latency during retrieval.

- Implement sharding for large indices, distributing them across multiple nodes to parallelize queries.

Combining Real-Time and Batch Processing

Certain workflows benefit from a hybrid approach. For example, real-time chatbots might fetch instant answers from a preloaded index while concurrently processing batch jobs to analyze overall session trends. LangChain's AsyncChain allows for asynchronous task execution, integrating seamlessly with LlamaIndex's APIs.

Deploying AI Solutions at Scale

Scaling AI applications is more than just deploying powerful models; it involves ensuring robustness, reliability, and cost-efficiency. This chapter focuses on best practices for deploying LangChain and LlamaIndex-powered solutions in production.

Scalable Infrastructure

Deploying AI systems on scalable infrastructure like Kubernetes or serverless platforms (AWS Lambda, Google Cloud Functions) ensures flexibility under varying loads. Using LangChain, developers can design chains that adapt to resource constraints dynamically. For instance:

- Use **adaptive batching** for inference requests during peak times.
- Implement **model fallback mechanisms** where a lighter model serves responses if the primary model is overloaded.

Monitoring and Debugging

Production systems need robust monitoring for metrics like latency, accuracy, and resource usage. LangChain provides hooks for integrating monitoring tools like Prometheus or Grafana. LlamaIndex offers logging capabilities to track retrieval performance and identify bottlenecks.

A practical debugging workflow might involve:

1. Capturing logs of query pipelines using LangChain's CallbackManager.

2. Analyzing retrieval logs from LlamaIndex for anomalies, such as poor relevance scores.

3. Using visualization tools to inspect embeddings or similarity metrics

Cost Optimization

Both LangChain and LlamaIndex provide mechanisms for cost control:

- **Optimizing API calls**: Use caching layers to store frequent query results, reducing reliance on external API invocations.

- **Index partitioning**: For LlamaIndex, partitioning large datasets ensures only relevant segments are queried, minimizing compute costs.

By implementing these strategies, developers can deploy robust and cost-effective AI systems at scale.

Chapter 4: LangChain Overview

LangChain is a powerful and versatile LLM framework known for its ability to create complex and interactive applications. Here's a closer look:

4.1 Core functionalities of LangChain

- **Chaining LLMs:** LangChain excels at chaining together multiple LLM interactions. This allows you to build applications with a natural conversational flow, where the LLM's response to one prompt informs the next one.

- **External Data Integration:** LangChain integrates seamlessly with external data sources like databases and APIs. This allows your application to access and process information beyond the LLM's internal knowledge base.

- **Long-term Memory:** LangChain can maintain a history of user interactions, enabling applications to adapt and respond based on context. Imagine a chatbot that remembers your preferences from previous interactions.

4.2 Advantages of LangChain

- **Flexibility:** LangChain's chaining capabilities and data integration features make it suitable for building a wide range of complex LLM applications.

- **Control Flow:** LangChain allows developers to define control flow within the application, including conditional statements and loops. This enables building applications with more intricate workflows.

- **Active Development:** LangChain is an actively maintained framework with a growing community, ensuring ongoing support and updates.

4.3 Limitations of LangChain

- **Complexity:** LangChain's flexibility comes with a steeper learning curve compared to simpler frameworks.

- **Computational Resources:** Building complex LLM applications with LangChain may require significant computational resources.

Chapter 5: LlamaIndex Overview

LlamaIndex takes a different approach, focusing on efficient search and retrieval of information relevant to LLM tasks. Here's what it offers:

5.1 Core functionalities of LlamaIndex

- **Information Indexing:** LlamaIndex excels at creating indexes of text data, allowing for fast and efficient retrieval of relevant information for the LLM. This improves the accuracy and focus of the LLM's responses.

- **Data Filtering and Ranking:** LlamaIndex can filter and rank retrieved information based on specific criteria, ensuring the LLM receives the most relevant data for its task.

- **Focus on Search Tasks:** LlamaIndex is specifically designed for applications where accurate retrieval of information is crucial.

5.2 Advantages of LlamaIndex

- **Efficiency:** LlamaIndex's indexing capabilities ensure fast and accurate retrieval of information, leading to efficient LLM performance.

- **Scalability:** LlamaIndex can handle large amounts of data efficiently, making it suitable for large-scale applications.
- **Ease of Use:** LlamaIndex has a simpler interface compared to some frameworks, making it easier to learn and use for specific search-oriented tasks.

5.3 Limitations of LlamaIndex

- **Limited Functionality:** LlamaIndex is primarily focused on search and retrieval. While it can be used for basic LLM interactions, it may not be suitable for building complex conversational applications.
- **Less Customization:** LlamaIndex offers less flexibility for controlling the LLM's behavior compared to frameworks like LangChain.

By understanding the strengths and weaknesses of both LangChain and LlamaIndex, developers can choose the right framework for their specific LLM application needs.

Orchestrating Multi-Agent Systems with LangChain

LangChain provides a framework for building systems where multiple AI agents collaborate to achieve complex objectives. Multi-agent orchestration leverages the strengths of specialized agents, such as retrieval bots, summarization bots, or decision-making bots, enabling seamless task execution.

Designing Agent Roles

To create a functional multi-agent system, defining clear roles for each agent is essential. For instance:

- **Retrieval Agent:** Queries LlamaIndex or external APIs to gather relevant information.
- **Processing Agent:** Analyzes and summarizes the retrieved data.
- **Decision Agent:** Evaluates the processed data to make actionable recommendations.

By defining these roles, the workflow becomes modular, allowing easy scaling or replacement of individual agents as needed.

Agent Communication Protocols

Agents require a robust mechanism to exchange data and coordinate actions. LangChain supports message passing between agents, ensuring structured interactions. For example:

- Use LangChain's Memory modules to store shared state across agents.
- Establish workflows with Chain objects that orchestrate sequential or parallel tasks.

Use Case: Multi-Agent Research Assistant

Imagine a research assistant that collects, synthesizes, and evaluates literature:

1. **Retrieval Agent:** Fetches research papers using LlamaIndex, prioritizing recency and relevance.
2. **Summarization Agent:** Extracts key findings and presents concise summaries.
3. **Validation Agent:** Checks the reliability of sources and identifies gaps in the literature.

By orchestrating these agents, users receive actionable insights with minimal manual effort.

Custom Embedding Strategies for Domain-Specific Tasks

Custom embeddings are crucial for fine-tuning LlamaIndex's performance in specialized domains. While pre-trained embeddings like OpenAI's or SentenceTransformers work well generally, domain-specific embeddings improve retrieval relevance significantly.

Creating Domain-Specific Embeddings

1. **Fine-Tune Pre-Trained Models:** Use domain-specific data (e.g., legal texts, medical records) to fine-tune embedding models. Hugging Face and TensorFlow offer straightforward pipelines for this.

2. **Generate Synthetic Data:** When real data is scarce, generate domain-relevant synthetic data to train or fine-tune embeddings.

3. **Evaluate Embedding Quality:** Use metrics like cosine similarity and information retrieval benchmarks to measure embedding performance.

Integrating Custom Embeddings with LlamaIndex

LlamaIndex supports custom embeddings through its CustomEmbedding class. Replace the default embedding logic with your model to align retrieval results with domain-specific needs.

python

Copy code

```
from llama_index.embeddings.custom import CustomEmbedding


class DomainEmbedding(CustomEmbedding):
    def embed_text(self, text: str) -> List[float]:
        return my_custom_model.encode(text)  # Replace with your embedding logic
```

Deploying these custom embeddings ensures that retrieval pipelines adapt to specialized requirements, whether in finance, healthcare, or technical documentation.

Complex Data Augmentation for Enhanced Model Performance

Data augmentation transforms training and retrieval datasets to improve AI model robustness and performance. Combining LangChain's augmentation tools with LlamaIndex's indexing pipelines, developers can create sophisticated workflows that prepare high-quality datasets.

Augmentation Techniques

1. **Paraphrasing:** Use LangChain to generate paraphrases of existing text, ensuring semantic diversity without altering core meaning.
2. **Noisy Data Injection:** Introduce controlled noise (e.g., typos, synonyms) to improve the model's ability to handle real-world inputs.
3. **Back-Translation:** Translate text into another language and back to generate diverse phrasing.

Augmentation in Retrieval Systems

For retrieval, augmenting both the query and the indexed data improves recall and precision. With LlamaIndex:

- Augment the query dynamically using LangChain's prompt chaining to rephrase or expand inputs.

- Index augmented documents alongside original documents to broaden the retrieval scope.

Use Case: Robust Question-Answering System

In a customer support context, data augmentation ensures the system understands varied user phrasing. For instance:

- Original Query: *"How can I reset my password?"*

- Augmented Queries: *"What are the steps for a password reset?"*, *"How to recover access to my account?"*

Augmenting queries during indexing and retrieval ensures comprehensive coverage, improving user satisfaction.

Distributed Retrieval and Indexing with LlamaIndex

As datasets grow, scaling retrieval pipelines becomes critical. LlamaIndex supports distributed architectures, enabling high-performance retrieval across vast datasets.

Partitioning Large Indices

Partitioning is the first step in distributed retrieval:

- Split datasets by topic, timestamp, or other logical segments.
- Assign partitions to separate nodes for parallel processing.

LlamaIndex's API allows for efficient partitioning and querying across shards:

python

Copy code

```python
indices = [LlamaIndex(partition) for partition in data_partitions]
def query_shards(query):
    results = [index.query(query) for index in indices]
    return aggregate_results(results)
```

Parallel Retrieval with LangChain

LangChain complements distributed retrieval by orchestrating parallel queries to multiple LlamaIndex instances. Using AsyncChain, developers can handle concurrent requests seamlessly.

Scalability Best Practices

1. **Precompute Embeddings:** Store precomputed embeddings to avoid redundant computations during runtime.
2. **Caching Layers:** Use caching to serve frequent queries instantly.
3. **Horizontal Scaling:** Add nodes dynamically as data grows, ensuring consistent performance.

Ethical AI Systems with LangChain and LlamaIndex

Ethics in AI extends beyond compliance—it's about creating systems that are transparent, fair, and reliable. LangChain and LlamaIndex provide tools to implement ethical best practices in generative AI systems.

Addressing Bias in Retrieval

LlamaIndex's metadata filtering allows for bias detection and mitigation. For instance, if a dataset overrepresents one demographic, apply filters to balance retrieval results. Use embeddings to detect semantic bias by analyzing patterns in similarity scores.

Ensuring Transparency

Transparency involves making AI decisions explainable:

- Use LangChain's Chain visualizations to map decision flows for auditing.
- Generate step-by-step explanations of responses, highlighting data sources and logic.

Mitigating Hallucinations

Hallucinations occur when AI generates plausible but incorrect outputs. To mitigate this:

1. Validate facts using external APIs or databases through LangChain's tool integrations.

2. Cross-reference results from multiple indices in LlamaIndex to ensure accuracy.

Building Trustworthy Applications

A robust feedback mechanism builds user trust. Implement LangChain's FeedbackChain to collect user inputs on system responses and use this data to refine future interactions.

By embedding ethical considerations into system design, developers can ensure their applications are responsible and user-focused.

Part 3: Choosing the Right Framework

Chapter 6: Feature Comparison: LangChain vs. LlamaIndex

Choosing the right LLM framework depends on the specific needs of your application. Here's a breakdown of LangChain and LlamaIndex to help you decide:

**Feature	LangChain	LlamaIndex**
Core Functionality	Chaining LLM interactions, data integration	Information indexing, search, retrieval
Strengths	Flexibility, control flow, long-term memory	Efficiency, scalability, ease of use
Weaknesses	Complexity, computational resources	Limited functionality, less customization

Ideal Use Cases	Complex chatbots, Virtual assistants,	Question answering systems, document summarization

6.1 Use cases for LangChain

- **A personalized learning assistant:** Imagine an LLM application that tutors students. LangChain would be ideal for building context and memory of a student's progress. The application could chain together LLM interactions to adapt explanations and questions based on the student's past performance.

- **A creative writing assistant:** LangChain's ability to integrate with external data sources could be used to build a writing assistant that accesses information relevant to the writer's topic. The LLM could then use this information to suggest ideas, provide feedback, or even co-author creative text formats.

6.2 Use cases for LlamaIndex

- **A legal research assistant:** For a lawyer building an LLM application for legal research, accuracy and efficiency are paramount.

LlamaIndex's indexing capabilities can quickly retrieve relevant legal documents based on a user's query, allowing the LLM to analyze and summarize the information effectively.

- **A customer support chatbot:** For a company building a chatbot to answer basic customer service questions, LlamaIndex's focus on search and retrieval is ideal. The chatbot can efficiently find the most relevant information from a knowledge base to answer user queries.

Chapter 7: Combining LangChain and LlamaIndex

While LangChain and LlamaIndex have distinct strengths, they can sometimes be combined for even more powerful applications.

- **Scenario:** Imagine building a sophisticated research assistant chatbot that can not only conversationally answer user questions but also efficiently retrieve and analyze relevant research articles.

- **Solution:** Combine LangChain's conversational capabilities with LlamaIndex's information retrieval power. LangChain can handle the user interaction, understanding the research topic and refining the query based on conversation. LlamaIndex can then efficiently search for relevant research articles, and LangChain can use this information to summarize the findings or answer the user's questions in a comprehensive way.

By understanding the unique functionalities of each framework and exploring creative combinations, developers can unlock the full potential of LLMs and build innovative applications.

Part 4: Building Your LLM Application

Since you might choose LangChain or LlamaIndex based on your needs,

we'll provide separate chapter outlines for each framework.

Chapter 8: Building a Sample Application with LangChain

8.1 Setting up your development environment

- Choosing your tools: There are various tools and libraries needed

  for LLM development. We'll outline some popular options (e.g.,

  Python programming language, specific LLM libraries, LangChain

  framework itself).

- Installation and configuration: We'll provide a step-by-step guide on

  installing and configuring these tools to work seamlessly with

  LangChain.

8.2 Building a Q&A chatbot with LangChain

- Application overview: We'll design a simple question-answering

  chatbot as an example. This chatbot will use LangChain to interact

  with an LLM and answer user questions in a conversational way.

- Code walkthrough: We'll break down the code for this application

  step-by-step, explaining how LangChain is used to:

- Handle user input and format it as prompts for the LLM.

- Interact with the LLM and retrieve responses.

- Manage conversation history and context using LangChain's memory capabilities.

- Generate natural language responses based on the LLM's output.

Chapter 9: Brief Overview of LlamaIndex

While you might be focusing on LangChain for this application, here's a brief introduction to LlamaIndex for completeness.

- **Core functionalities:** A short recap of LlamaIndex's strengths, focusing on information indexing, search, and retrieval for LLM tasks.

- **Use cases:** A few examples of applications where LlamaIndex would be a strong choice (e.g., document summarization tools, information retrieval assistants).

Case Study 1: Enhancing Legal Research with LangChain and LlamaIndex

Background:

A mid-sized law firm struggled with the time-intensive process of legal research. Associates spent hours sifting through case law, regulations, and client documents to prepare for cases. The firm sought a solution to automate and enhance research efficiency without compromising accuracy.

Solution:

By integrating **LangChain** and **LlamaIndex**, the firm created a custom legal research assistant that combined text retrieval, summarization, and decision-making capabilities.

1. **Building the Knowledge Base:**

   Using LlamaIndex, the firm indexed case law, statutory regulations, and client contracts. They employed custom embeddings fine-tuned on legal texts to ensure domain-specific relevance.

2. **Query Handling:**

   LangChain's prompt engineering enabled the assistant to interpret complex legal queries. For example, "Find precedents where breach of contract was ruled favorably for the defendant in California" was parsed into actionable tasks.

3. **Multi-Step Reasoning:**

   LangChain orchestrated the assistant's reasoning process. It retrieved relevant case laws, summarized key points, and evaluated their applicability to the user's context.

4. **Ethical Safeguards:**

   To prevent hallucinations or biased retrieval, the system was programmed to prioritize authoritative sources and flag conflicting

results.

Impact:

The firm reduced research time by 70% while improving the

comprehensiveness of legal briefs. Associates reported a more efficient

workflow, enabling them to focus on case strategy rather than document

review.

Case Study 2: Personalized Education Content Generation for EdTech

Background:

An EdTech startup wanted to create personalized learning experiences for students. The challenge was generating educational content tailored to varying skill levels, learning styles, and languages.

Solution:

The company used LangChain for content generation and LlamaIndex to manage a repository of educational materials, including textbooks, research papers, and past student queries.

1. **Dynamic Content Creation:**

   LangChain leveraged prompts that incorporated user profiles to generate personalized lesson plans, quizzes, and study materials.

2. **Adaptive Retrieval:**

   LlamaIndex retrieved relevant materials based on the current learning objectives and integrated them into LangChain's generative process.

3. **Feedback Loop:**

   LangChain's FeedbackChain allowed students to rate the usefulness

   of generated content. This feedback was used to fine-tune the

   system over time.

Impact:

Students demonstrated a 20% improvement in test scores after using the

platform for three months. Teachers appreciated the automated lesson

plans, reducing their workload significantly.

Case Study 3: Financial Forecasting for Asset Management

Background:

A global asset management firm needed an AI-powered system to provide accurate financial forecasts and portfolio recommendations.

Solution:

The firm combined LangChain and LlamaIndex to analyze financial data, news, and historical trends.

1. **Data Integration:**

   Financial reports, market news, and economic indicators were indexed using LlamaIndex. Custom embeddings optimized for financial jargon improved retrieval quality.

2. **Scenario Analysis:**

   LangChain powered simulations for various economic scenarios, providing portfolio recommendations based on projected outcomes

3. **Transparency:**

   To enhance trust, the system included explainability features, detailing the rationale behind each forecast.

Impact:

Portfolio performance improved by 12% annually, and clients reported higher confidence in investment strategies due to AI-driven insights.

Case Study 4: Conversational Healthcare Assistant

Background:

A healthcare provider wanted to build a conversational assistant to answer patient queries, schedule appointments, and provide preliminary diagnoses.

Solution:

The provider developed the assistant using LangChain for conversational logic and LlamaIndex to retrieve medical knowledge.

1. **Knowledge Base Creation:**

   LlamaIndex indexed medical guidelines, drug databases, and FAQs.

2. **Context-Aware Conversations:**

   LangChain ensured the assistant understood patient intent and provided accurate, empathetic responses.

3. **Regulatory Compliance:**

   The system adhered to HIPAA guidelines, ensuring data privacy and security.

Impact:

Patients received instant, reliable answers to their queries, reducing call center traffic by 40% and improving satisfaction scores.

Case Study 5: AI-Powered Recruitment Platform

Background:

A recruitment agency wanted to streamline candidate sourcing and matching by automating the process with AI.

Solution:

LangChain and LlamaIndex were used to build an intelligent recruitment assistant.

1. **Candidate Matching:**

   Resumes and job descriptions were indexed in LlamaIndex. LangChain analyzed the similarity between job requirements and candidate skills.

2. **Conversational Engagement:**

   LangChain enabled natural conversations with candidates,

gathering additional information like salary expectations and availability.

3. **Bias Mitigation:**

   The system flagged potential biases in job descriptions or candidate evaluations to promote fairness.

Impact:

The agency reduced time-to-hire by 50% and improved client satisfaction with more accurate candidate matches.

Case Study 6: Retail Chatbot for E-Commerce Personalization

Background:

A major e-commerce platform wanted to enhance customer experience with a chatbot that provided personalized product recommendations.

Solution:

LangChain handled conversational logic, while LlamaIndex managed product catalogs and customer interaction data.

1. **Personalized Recommendations:**

   The chatbot analyzed browsing history and preferences to suggest products.

2. **Real-Time Updates:**

   LlamaIndex dynamically updated with new inventory and promotions.

3. **Seamless Integration:**

   The chatbot integrated with payment and order tracking systems for end-to-end customer support.

Impact:

Sales increased by 18%, and customers praised the intuitive shopping experience.

Case Study 7: Automated Compliance Monitoring in Banking

Background:

A bank needed an AI system to monitor transactions for compliance with AML (Anti-Money Laundering) regulations.

Solution:

LangChain and LlamaIndex powered an automated monitoring system.

1. **Transaction Analysis:**

   LlamaIndex indexed historical transactions and compliance rules. LangChain flagged anomalies in real time.

2. **Investigation Assistance:**

   The system summarized flagged transactions, highlighting reasons for suspicion.

3. **Audit Trails:**

   LangChain maintained detailed records of all system actions for

   audits.   .

Impact:

The bank reduced false positives by 30% and improved regulatory

compliance.

Case Study 8: Academic Research Assistance

Background:

A university wanted an AI tool to assist researchers in literature reviews

and citation generation.

Solution:

LangChain and LlamaIndex provided a comprehensive research assistant.

1. **Literature Retrieval:**

   LlamaIndex retrieved papers based on research topics.

2. **Summary Generation:**

   LangChain summarized key findings and highlighted trends.

3. **Citation Management:**

   The assistant auto-generated citations in multiple formats.

Impact:

Researchers completed reviews 50% faster and cited more relevant

sources.

Case Study 9: Media Monitoring for Brand Reputation

Background:

A PR agency needed to monitor media mentions for their clients and

assess public sentiment.

Solution:

LangChain analyzed sentiment in real time, while LlamaIndex indexed

articles, tweets, and posts.

1. **Sentiment Analysis:**

   The system flagged positive or negative trends in client mentions.

2. **Crisis Alerts:**

   LangChain sent alerts for potentially damaging mentions, enabling

   rapid response.

Impact:

Clients reported improved crisis management and proactive reputation

building.

Case Study 10: Supply Chain Optimization

Background:

A logistics company wanted to optimize supply chain operations using AI

insights.

Solution:

LangChain and LlamaIndex analyzed supply chain data, including

inventory levels, shipping routes, and delivery schedules.

1. **Route Optimization:**

   LangChain identified cost-effective routes.

2. **Inventory Management:**

   LlamaIndex predicted stock shortages and suggested

   replenishments.

3. **Real-Time Insights:**

   The system provided live updates on shipment statuses.

Impact:

The company reduced logistics costs by 15% and improved delivery

timelines.

Advanced Prompt Engineering with LangChain

Prompt engineering is the cornerstone of building effective AI-driven workflows, especially when combining **LangChain** with other tools. Advanced techniques go beyond simple query construction, enabling nuanced, context-aware interactions tailored for specific applications. This chapter explores how to optimize prompts for multi-step reasoning, dynamic workflows, and user-specific contexts.

Dynamic Prompting

Dynamic prompting involves creating adaptable queries based on real-time data or user input. For instance, in customer support chatbots, prompts can be adjusted based on the user's previous interactions or profile data.

- **Techniques for Dynamic Prompts:**
  - **Template-based Prompts:** Use placeholders to dynamically populate specific details.
  - **Conditional Logic:** Include branches in the prompt workflow based on user responses.

- o **Embedded Queries:** Leverage LlamaIndex to fetch context-specific data and embed it within the LangChain prompt.

- **Example Workflow:**

Consider a healthcare assistant tasked with diagnosing symptoms The system retrieves patient history from a medical database (via LlamaIndex) and generates a tailored query:

vbnet

Copy code

Given the patient's history of hypertension and their reported symptoms of chest pain and shortness of breath, provide a potential diagnosis and recommended next steps.

Optimizing Prompts for Long-Form Tasks

LangChain supports handling complex, multi-turn interactions where tasks evolve over time. Achieving this requires breaking down prompts into modular components.

- **Chained Prompts:**

Modularize tasks into smaller, interdependent prompts. For instance, in a research assistant application:

1. Retrieve relevant papers from LlamaIndex.

2. Generate a summary for each paper.

3. Combine summaries into a cohesive report.

- **Memory Integration:**

  Use LangChain's memory capabilities to retain context across interactions, ensuring continuity in user conversations.

Error-Resistant Prompts

When using AI systems in high-stakes scenarios, error tolerance is crucial. LangChain allows fallback mechanisms to refine or reattempt prompts based on initial outcomes.

- **Debugging Tools:**

  Test prompts extensively in sandbox environments to identify weak points. Tools like LangChain's PromptTester streamline this process.

- **Adaptive Feedback Loops:**

  Incorporate user feedback to improve prompts over time, particularly in applications like education or content generation.

Applications of Advanced Prompt Engineering

From multi-modal workflows to enterprise-grade solutions, advanced prompt engineering unlocks new possibilities. Businesses can achieve greater automation, precision, and personalization by leveraging these techniques effectively.

Integrating LangChain with Enterprise Systems

Enterprises operate with diverse, interconnected ecosystems of software and data. Integrating **LangChain** and **LlamaIndex** into these systems requires careful planning, scalable architecture, and robust APIs to deliver meaningful results. This chapter delves into best practices for enterprise integration, highlighting real-world use cases.

API-First Design

Modern enterprises rely on API-driven workflows for seamless integration between systems. LangChain provides out-of-the-box support for API integrations, making it suitable for embedding into existing workflows.

- **Example:**

  An enterprise HR system integrates LangChain to automate candidate screening. A custom API fetches resumes, analyzes them for key skills using LangChain, and updates the applicant tracking system with ranked recommendations.

Multi-System Workflows

Enterprises often use multiple tools for different purposes. LangChain can serve as the central orchestrator.

- **Data Retrieval with LlamaIndex:**

  Fetch data from various sources like CRM databases, ERP systems, or third-party APIs.

- **Task Delegation:**

  Assign specialized subtasks to external systems, such as sending notifications via Slack or updating records in Salesforce.

Security and Compliance

Integrating AI into enterprise systems requires strict adherence to security and compliance standards.

- **Data Encryption:**

  Encrypt sensitive data during both retrieval and processing phases.

- **Access Controls:**

  Implement role-based access for LangChain workflows to prevent unauthorized usage.

- **Compliance Frameworks:**

  Ensure adherence to standards like GDPR or HIPAA, especially when processing personal or sensitive data.

Scalability Challenges

Scaling LangChain workflows across large organizations introduces challenges in resource allocation and latency management.

- **Distributed Processing:**

  Use distributed systems to parallelize tasks, ensuring minimal downtime during high-demand periods.

- **Performance Monitoring:**

  Employ monitoring tools to track API latency, error rates, and throughput.

Building Domain-Specific Language Models with LlamaIndex

Domain-specific applications require highly tailored language models capable of understanding industry jargon, nuanced contexts, and unique datasets. By combining **LangChain** and **LlamaIndex**, developers can build and deploy these specialized models effectively.

Dataset Curation and Preparation

The foundation of any domain-specific model is a high-quality dataset.

- **Source Selection:**

  Identify authoritative sources within the domain. For example, medical models may rely on PubMed, clinical guidelines, and electronic health records.

- **Data Annotation:**

  Employ domain experts to annotate datasets, ensuring accuracy and relevance.

Custom Indexing with LlamaIndex

LlamaIndex facilitates indexing of diverse data types, enabling rapid access to domain-specific knowledge.

- **Hierarchical Indexing:**

  Organize data hierarchically to reflect domain structures, such as

  chapters in textbooks or sections in legal statutes.

- **Embedding Optimization:**

  Fine-tune embeddings to capture domain-specific semantics,

  improving retrieval relevance.

Fine-Tuning Pre-Trained Models

Fine-tuning involves adapting a general-purpose language model to a

specific domain.

- **Transfer Learning:**

  Start with a general LLM like GPT-3 or T5 and fine-tune it using

  curated datasets.

- **Training Frameworks:**

  Use tools like PyTorch or TensorFlow in conjunction with LangChain

  for smooth integration into the development pipeline.

Evaluation Metrics

Assessing domain-specific models requires tailored metrics.

- **Accuracy in Retrieval Tasks:**

  Measure precision and recall for tasks like document retrieval or information extraction.

- **Contextual Understanding:**

  Evaluate the model's ability to interpret nuanced queries, using benchmarks specific to the domain.

Deployment and Maintenance

Deploying a domain-specific model is just the beginning. Ongoing maintenance ensures the model remains effective as data evolves.

- **Monitoring Performance:**

  Track metrics like response accuracy and user satisfaction.

- **Regular Updates:**

  Periodically re-train the model with new data to incorporate recent developments in the domain.

By leveraging LangChain and LlamaIndex, developers can create robust, domain-specific language models that cater to specialized industries like healthcare, finance, law, and education.

Real-Time Decision Making with LangChain and LlamaIndex

Real-time decision-making is critical in applications such as financial trading, supply chain optimization, and emergency response systems. Combining **LangChain** and **LlamaIndex** enables developers to build systems that process vast amounts of data, generate insights, and recommend actions with minimal latency. This chapter focuses on designing, implementing, and optimizing such systems.

Core Components of Real-Time Systems

To achieve real-time performance, the following components are essential:

- **Fast Data Ingestion:**
  Use LlamaIndex to index streaming data sources, such as IoT sensors, social media feeds, or financial tickers.

- **Low-Latency Processing:**
  LangChain's modular architecture enables swift execution of decision workflows. Pair this with highly efficient APIs for data retrieval and model inference.

- **Scalable Infrastructure:**

  Leverage cloud platforms with auto-scaling capabilities to handle

  fluctuating workloads.

Real-Time Use Cases

1. **Fraud Detection in Banking:**

   Monitor transactions in real time to detect anomalies using pre-

   trained models integrated into LangChain workflows.

   - Example: Analyze transaction metadata (location, time,

     amount) using LlamaIndex and flag deviations from typical

     patterns.

2. **Dynamic Pricing in E-Commerce:**

   Adjust product prices based on market trends, competitor activity,

   and inventory levels.

   - Example: Continuously retrieve competitor pricing data, feed

     it into LangChain, and compute optimized pricing strategies.

3. **Disaster Response Coordination:**

   Use social media data and emergency communication systems to

   direct resources effectively.

- Example: Extract location and severity information from real-time social media posts indexed via LlamaIndex.

Designing Real-Time Pipelines

1. **Data Stream Integration:**

   Integrate live data feeds into LlamaIndex. For instance, connect to APIs like Twitter for sentiment analysis or news sources for event monitoring.

2. **Decision Workflows in LangChain:**

   Define modular workflows capable of executing sequential and parallel tasks.

   - **Sequential:** A fraud detection system might first analyze transaction history before flagging risky accounts.

   - **Parallel:** A disaster response system could simultaneously assess multiple data streams (social media, weather updates, emergency services).

3. **Caching and Pre-Processing:**

   To reduce latency, cache frequently accessed data and pre-process raw information into structured formats.

Advanced Optimization Techniques

1. **Distributed Processing:**

   Utilize distributed frameworks like Apache Kafka or Spark Streaming for data preprocessing, which feeds into LangChain workflows.

2. **Asynchronous Operations:**

   Asynchronous APIs ensure that workflows do not bottleneck while waiting for slow processes like external API calls.

3. **Model Quantization:**

   For faster inference, deploy quantized versions of language models that retain accuracy while reducing computational requirements.

4. **Edge Computing:**

   Process critical data closer to the source using edge devices, reducing round-trip latency to cloud servers.

Evaluation and Monitoring

Real-time systems require robust evaluation to ensure reliability and effectiveness.

- **Key Metrics:**

- **Latency:** Measure end-to-end response time from data ingestion to decision output.

- **Throughput:** Track the number of decisions processed per second.

- **Accuracy:** Monitor decision outcomes and refine models to improve precision.

- **Monitoring Tools:**

  Use APM (Application Performance Monitoring) tools like New Relic or Datadog to track system health and identify bottlenecks.

Challenges in Real-Time Decision Making

1. **Handling Data Volume:**

   Large-scale systems generate enormous data volumes, requiring scalable indexing and efficient retrieval strategies.

2. **Maintaining Accuracy at Speed:**

   Balancing real-time performance with decision quality necessitates advanced tuning of both models and workflows.

3. **Resilience to Failures:**

   Implement failover mechanisms to ensure uninterrupted operation during component failures or unexpected data surges.

Real-World Implementation

Consider a supply chain management system:

- **Problem:** Optimize delivery routes based on real-time traffic, weather, and inventory data.

- **Solution:**

    o Use LlamaIndex to continuously fetch and index live traffic and weather data.

    o Design LangChain workflows to compute the most efficient routes, factoring in delivery deadlines and costs.

    o Deploy the system on a cloud infrastructure with auto-scaling to handle peak demand periods.

This system not only reduces delivery times but also minimizes costs, ensuring high customer satisfaction and operational efficiency.

By combining LangChain's modularity with LlamaIndex's data handling capabilities, developers can craft sophisticated real-time decision-making systems for a wide array of industries.

Part 5: Conclusion

Chapter 10: The Future of LLM Frameworks

- **Advancements in LLM technology:** A discussion on how LLMs themselves are expected to evolve, becoming more powerful and versatile.

- **Evolving LLM frameworks:** We'll explore how LLM frameworks like LangChain and LlamaIndex might adapt to these advancements, offering even more functionalities and capabilities for developers.

- **Impact on various industries:** A glimpse into how powerful LLM applications built with these frameworks could revolutionize various sectors like education, customer service, and scientific research.

This structure provides a roadmap for building your LLM application, along with an understanding of the complementary strengths of LangChain and LlamaIndex.

www.ingramcontent.com/pod-product-compliance
Lightning Source LLC
LaVergne TN
LVHW051608050326
832903LV00033B/4400